New Hampshire

Niels R. Jensen

Visit us at
www.abdopublishing.com

Published by ABDO Publishing Company, 8000 West 78th Street, Suite 310, Edina, Minnesota 55439 USA. Copyright ©2010 by Abdo Consulting Group, Inc. International copyrights reserved in all countries. No part of this book may be reproduced in any form without written permission from the publisher. The Checkerboard Library™ is a trademark and logo of ABDO Publishing Company.

Printed in the United States.

Editor: John Hamilton
Graphic Design: Sue Hamilton
Cover Illustration: Neil Klinepier
Cover Photo: iStock
Interior Photo Credits: Alamy, Anheuser-Busch Companies, AP Images, Comstock, Corbis, Getty, Granger Collection, Gunter Küchler, iStock Photo, Library of Congress, Lisa Jacobs, Mile High Maps, Mountain High Maps, NASA, New Hampshire Historical Society/Joseph Blackburn, One Mile Up, Peter Arnold Inc., and Rob Gallagher.
Statistics: State population statistics taken from 2008 U.S. Census Bureau estimates. City and town population statistics taken from July 1, 2007, U.S. Census Bureau estimates. Land and water area statistics taken from 2000 Census, U.S. Census Bureau.

Manufactured with paper containing at least 10% post-consumer waste

Library of Congress Cataloging-in-Publication Data

Jensen, Niels R., 1949-
  New Hampshire / Niels R. Jensen.
      p. cm. -- (The United States)
  Includes index.
  ISBN 978-1-60453-664-5
  1. New Hampshire--Juvenile literature. I. Title.

F34.3.J46 2009
974.2--dc22

2008051720

Table of Contents

The Granite State

People first came to New Hampshire because of the land's great natural resources. There were fish, farmland, tall trees, and water power. As the state developed, the people wanted to govern themselves. They wanted freedom. It was the first of the American colonies to declare independence from England.

New Hampshire moved quickly to strengthen voting rights. The state removed land ownership requirement in order for people to vote. It stopped taxing people for religious purposes. New Hampshire today is the first state to hold presidential primaries to select the nation's Republican and Democratic candidates.

New Hampshire's industries have modernized, but its great natural wonders bring many visitors to the state.

Many people visit New Hampshire
to see its beautiful natural wonders.

Name: Named after Hampshire, a county in England

State Capital: Concord, population 42,392

Date of Statehood: June 21, 1788 (9th state)

Population: 1,315,809 (41st-most populous state)

Area (Total Land and Water): 9,350 square miles (24,216 sq km), 46th-largest state

Largest City: Manchester, population 108,874

Nickname: The Granite State

Motto: Live Free or Die

State Bird: Purple Finch

State Flower: Purple Lilac

Franklin Pierce

State Rock: Granite

State Tree: White Birch

State Song: "Old New Hampshire"

Highest Point: Mt. Washington, 6,288 feet (1,917 m)

Lowest Point: Atlantic Ocean, 0 ft. (0 m)

Average July Temperature: 68°F (20°C)

Record High Temperature: 106°F (41°C) Nashua, July 4, 1911

Average January Temperature: 19°F (-7°C)

Record Low Temperature: -47°F (-44°C), Mt. Washington, January 29, 1934

Average Annual Precipitation: 42 inches (107 cm)

Number of U.S. Senators: 2

Number of U.S. Representatives: 2

U.S. Presidents Born in New Hampshire: Franklin Pierce (1804-1869)

U.S. Postal Service Abbreviation: NH

Geography

The White Mountains of New Hampshire are part of the Appalachian Mountains. They rose up more than 100 million years ago.

Later, ice-age glaciers one mile (1.6 km) thick scraped the entire state. They left behind rocks, gravel, and sand. When the ice melted, its water carved valleys and created lakes.

There is plenty of water in New Hampshire today. The state is sometimes called the Mother of Rivers. It has about 40,000 miles (64,374 km) of rivers and streams. The Androscoggin, Cocheco, Connecticut, Merrimack, Saco, Salmon Falls, Pemigewasset, Piscataqua, and Winnipesaukee Rivers all begin in New Hampshire.

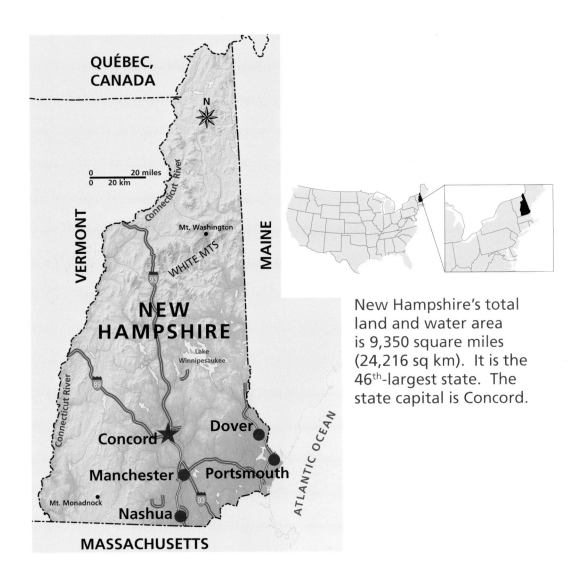

QUÉBEC, CANADA

N

0   20 miles
0   20 km

Connecticut River

VERMONT

Mt. Washington

WHITE MTS

93

NEW HAMPSHIRE

Lake Winnipesaukee

MAINE

Connecticut River

89

Concord

Dover

Manchester

Portsmouth

Mt. Monadnock

93

Nashua

ATLANTIC OCEAN

MASSACHUSETTS

New Hampshire's total land and water area is 9,350 square miles (24,216 sq km). It is the 46th-largest state. The state capital is Concord.

Lake Winnipesaukee is 21 miles (34 km) long. It is the biggest lake in New Hampshire. Many people come to boat, sail, and swim in its waters.

The state also has about 1,300 lakes and ponds. Lake Winnipesaukee is the largest. Its waters cover 72 square miles (186 sq km). It has more than 250 islands. The lake is popular with tourists.

The White Mountains region of New Hampshire has rocky peaks, narrow valleys, and streams. The Presidential Range is part of the White Mountains.

It includes Mt. Washington, which is 6,288 feet (1,917 m) tall. It is the highest peak in New England. It is famous for its harsh weather.

There are woods to the north of the White Mountains. To the south are uplands that include lakes, fertile soil, and mountains. Mt. Monadnock is a National Natural Landmark. It is one of the world's most-climbed peaks.

The southeastern part of New Hampshire is a lowland by the Atlantic Ocean. There are sandy beaches, rocky ledges, and tidal wetlands. The state has only 18 miles (29 km) of coastline. It is the shortest coastline in the country.

New Hampshire's southeastern border is the Atlantic Ocean.

Climate and Weather

New Hampshire has a humid continental climate. There are large swings in daily and seasonal temperatures. There are four distinct seasons.

Different air masses meet in the region. Cold and dry air comes from Canada. Warm, moist air comes from the south. Cool, damp air comes from the Atlantic Ocean. The sea breezes, ocean currents, and tall mountains all have an effect on the state's weather. There can be thunderstorms, blizzards, and heavy downpours. Luckily, tornados are rare.

Mt. Washington has some of the world's worst weather. There is snow, ice, and fog. In 1934, the thermometer dropped to -47° Fahrenheit (-44°C).

It was a record cold temperature for the state. The fastest wind speed recorded on the mountain was a world record 231 miles per hour (372 kph).

A man hikes Mt. Washington in the winter. Some of the worst weather in the world occurs in this area.

Plants and Animals

Forests cover 84 percent of New Hampshire. That is about 5 million acres (2 million ha) of forestland. New Hampshire forests are a prized resource for wood industries, recreation, and tourism. The forests also provide habitat for wildlife. The many local trees include maple, birch, beech, ash, aspen, pine, spruce, and oak. New Hampshire is famous for its spectacular fall colors. The leaves turn bright red, yellow, and orange.

There are about 500 types of animals in the state. The list includes black bear, beaver, bobcat, coyote, deer, fisher, fox, raccoon, skunk, and snowshoe hare. Route 3, which runs north to the Canadian border, is known as Moose Alley. Moose can cause accidents, but the road is popular with tourists, who like to take pictures of the big animals.

Tourists stop to photograph a moose near Pittsburg, New Hampshire.

Skunk

Snowshoe Rabbit

Red Fox

New Hampshire is a wonderful place for bird watching. The state's many birds include cardinals, woodpeckers, chickadees, ducks, eagles, falcons, geese, gulls, hawks, herons, loons, owls, and sandpipers.

Once almost gone from New Hampshire, peregrine falcons have made a comeback.

To help the loon population, floating nesting islands have been made in New Hampshire's Lake Winnipesaukee.

The state's waters include bass, bullhead, carp, cod, haddock, herring, mackerel, perch, pike, salmon, trout, walleye, whitefish, and many others. There are also crabs, lobster, mussels, scallops, and shrimp.

Humpback, minke, and pilot whales are seen in the ocean. There are also dolphins and porpoises.

Salmon are stocked in many New Hampshire lakes and rivers.

History

Native Americans stand on a hill overlooking Lake Winnipesaukee.

There have been people in New Hampshire for 12,000 years. About 3,000 years ago, Native Americans began planting corn, beans, squash, and tobacco. Villages developed.

Algonquian Native Americans lived in the New Hampshire area when the first English and French explorers came in the early 1600s. John Smith of England surveyed New Hampshire's coast in 1614.

In 1622, English Captain John Mason was allowed to develop land in the area that is now New Hampshire. In 1623, he sent colonists to build fishing settlements at the mouth of the Piscataqua River. In 1629, Mason named the area the Province of New Hampshire.

The early fishing, lumber, and fur trades were important. Farming developed. People from Massachusetts began moving to the area. In

Settlers came to New Hampshire in the 1600s.

1641, Massachusetts got control of the land. However, in 1680, England's King Charles II made New Hampshire a separate royal colony.

Relations with Native Americans soured. Strong log houses known as garrisons were built on high ground. Members of the Penacook tribe made a surprise attack on the colonists in 1689. Today, the attack is known as the Cochecho Massacre.

In 1740, England's King George II settled a border disagreement between New Hampshire and Massachusetts. Benning Wentworth became the first royal governor in 1741.

The aftermath of the French and Indian War (1754-1763) created conflict between England and its American colonies. In 1774, colonists raided

John Sullivan of the Continental Congress captured Fort William and Mary from the English in December 1774. The raiders took 200 kegs of gunpowder for the American war effort.

guns and ammunition at Fort William and Mary. On January 5, 1776, New Hampshire became the first of the American colonies to declare itself independent from England.

Members of New Hampshire's militia fought in the American Revolution (1775-1783), but there were not any battles in the state. Navy and privateer ships were built at Portsmouth. They included John Paul Jones' frigate, the USS *Ranger*.

During the American Revolution, John Paul Jones captained the New Hampshire-built USS *Ranger*.

On June 21, 1788, New Hampshire approved the United States Constitution. It was the ninth state to ratify the Constitution. New Hampshire's vote made the Constitution the official law of the United States.

The War of 1812 (1812-1815) was unpopular in New Hampshire because it damaged trade. Shipping stopped. American privateers again sailed out from Portsmouth.

The state saw major industrial growth in the following decades. Textile mills and railways were built. Many people moved to New Hampshire to work.

There was strong anti-slavery support. During the Civil War (1861-1865), New Hampshire sent nearly 35,000 soldiers. They fought at Chancellorsville, Cold Harbor, Gettysburg, and other important battles.

Logging camp

Quarry

New Hampshire's economy became even more centered on manufacturing in the years after the Civil War. Lumbering boomed. Quarries were opened.

However, New Hampshire farms struggled because of competition from states in the Midwest. Many farms were abandoned.

After World War I (1914-1918), some textile mills were unable to compete with factories in America's Southern states. The communities switched to making other products. The Great Depression during the 1930s was a severe hardship. Many people lost their jobs. The state eventually recovered. Today, New Hampshire once again has a strong local economy.

New Hampshire turned to tourism to help with the state's economy. Skiing became popular in the state.

Did You Know?

- When New Hampshire was a British colony, its huge pine trees were the property of the king. Many were prized as masts for ships in the Royal Navy.

- There is a mysterious collection of rock walls and chambers at Salem, New Hampshire. It is sometimes called America's Stonehenge. It is claimed to have some of the oldest human-made structures in the nation.

- One team of the famous Clydesdale horses of the Anheuser-Busch Brewery is based in Merrimack.

- The state claims a number of skiing "firsts." The nation's first ski club was formed at Berlin, New Hampshire, in 1882. The first intercollegiate ski meet took place at Dartmouth College in 1914. The first American slalom race took place in the state in 1925, and the first American downhill race in 1926.

- Some people say Thorvald's Rock in Hampton is a Viking-era rune stone. Local legend says the stone marks the final resting place of Thorvald, the brother of Viking explorer Leif Ericsson. Historians disagree whether the stone is authentic or not.

People

Ken Burns (1953-) is an American filmmaker living in New Hampshire. He is best known for his documentaries about the Civil War, Lewis and Clark, and World War II. Burns often uses historical pictures and letters to tell a story.

Robert Frost (1874-1963) was a famous American poet. His works include *The Road Not Taken* and *Stopping by Woods on a Snowy Evening*. In 1961, he spoke at President John F. Kennedy's inauguration. Frost lived for many years in New Hampshire, where he wrote and taught.

Horace Greeley (1811-1872) was a leading newspaper editor. He used his *New York Tribune* to push reform, anti-slavery, and Western settlement. He was a presidential candidate in 1872. Greeley was born in Amherst, New Hampshire.

Christa McAuliffe (1948-1986) was a teacher at Concord High School, in Concord, New Hampshire. She was selected for the NASA Teacher In Space Project. She tragically died with all her crewmates aboard the space shuttle *Challenger.* The shuttle exploded soon after launch on January 28, 1986.

Adam Sandler (1966-) is an award-winning comedian, actor, musician, and film producer. He has worked on more than 30 films. He was with *Saturday Night Live* from 1990 to 1995. Sandler spent most of his childhood in Manchester, New Hampshire.

Alan B. Shepard, Jr. (1923-1998) piloted the *Freedom 7* Mercury mission on May 5, 1961. He became the first American, and the second person, to travel in space. In 1971, he commanded the *Apollo 14* mission to the moon. He was the first person to hit a golf ball on the surface of the moon. Shepard was born in Derry, New Hampshire.

David H. Souter (1939-) served as a justice of the United States Supreme Court from 1990 to 2009. He was born in Melrose, Massachusetts. When he was 11, he and his family moved to Weare, New Hampshire, where he still lives today. Souter likes to go mountain climbing in his home state.

Daniel Webster (1782-1852) was a United States secretary of state, congressman, and senator during the first part of the 1800s. He negotiated the eastern border between the United States and Canada. Webster was a skilled lawyer and convincing speaker. He was born in Salisbury, New Hampshire.

Cities

Concord became New Hampshire's capital in 1808. Its population is 42,392. The city was once a center of furniture making, granite quarrying, and textile manufacturing. It was also a center of railroad activity. Today, health care, insurance, and printing are the most important industries in Concord.

Dover was founded in 1623. It is the oldest lasting settlement in New Hampshire. The falls of the Cocheco River provided water power during the Industrial Revolution. The city was a leading producer of textiles. The old mills are now used for offices, retail space, and restaurants. Dover's population is 28,775.

Manchester is New Hampshire's largest city. Its population is 108,874. The city developed on the banks of the Merrimack River, which supplied power to mills. Cloth, fire engines, locomotives, paper, and shoes were made here. Today, the city relies on banking and retail services. It is also home to several colleges.

Nashua is New Hampshire's second-largest city. It has a population of 86,837. It was a former fur trade post and mill town. Today, important industries include high technology and defense. The Boston Air Route Traffic Control Center is located here.

Portsmouth is a seaport and tourist destination. Its population is 20,495. It grew wealthy from shipping, lumbering, shipbuilding, and fishing. The city was the colonial capital from 1679, but the government was moved to Exeter, New Hampshire, during the American Revolution (1775-1783).

Transportation

Manchester-Boston Regional Airport handles about four million passengers each year. It is the largest airport in New Hampshire. The other two big airports are Lebanon Municipal Airport and Portsmouth International Airport at Pease.

New Hampshire has about 17,000 miles (27,359 km) of roads. The main interstate highways are I-89, I-93, and I-95.

Portsmouth is New Hampshire's main harbor. It handles bulk cargo, container ships, passenger vessels, and commercial fishing boats.

A shipyard in Portsmouth, New Hampshire.

The Mount Washington Cog Railway pushes visitors up the mountain.

Freight trains operate on about 500 miles (805 km) of track in New Hampshire. The Mount Washington Cog Railway is very unusual. Powered by old steam locomotives, the trains climb to the top by using a toothed-rack rail.

Natural Resources

There are 4,166 farms in New Hampshire. The greatest income is from greenhouse and nursery plants, dairy, and apples. Farms also produce a large amount of berries, vegetables, honey, and maple syrup.

In times past, New Hampshire had many more farms than today. Farms located on the state's stony hills could not compete with the fertile plains of the Midwest. Farms were abandoned, and trees now cover many hillsides.

Forest-based manufacturing is an important business in New Hampshire. Some of the wood is used for paper and energy production. Christmas trees are also grown in the state.

New Hampshire's nickname is The Granite State. There are quarries in Coos, Hillsborough, and Merrimack Counties.

A University of New Hampshire organic farming professor leads a herd of cattle to pasture at the Burley-Demerrit Farm in Lee, New Hampshire. Organic farming uses Earth-friendly practices instead of chemicals.

Industry

New Hampshire's industries often developed where rivers provided water power and easy transportation. There were many mills. The manufacturing of cotton and wool cloth was especially huge.

Today, the state makes about $2.3 billion worth of goods. Appliances, chemicals, electronics, machinery, paper, and plastics are among its products. Some of New Hampshire's largest businesses include Fisher Scientific, The Timberland Company, and PC Connection.

Tourism is a major part of the state's economy. Approximately 67,000 people are employed in New Hampshire's tourism industry.

In the past, the state's vast forests supplied wood for the shipyards at Portsmouth. Cargo ships and U.S. Navy vessels were built here. That shipbuilding tradition continues at the Portsmouth Naval Shipyard on the border with Maine.

New Hampshire's forests have been logged for use in shipbuilding and paper mills. Today, many of the beautiful forests boost the state's economy by bringing tourists to New Hampshire.

Sports

Hiking and backpacking are very popular outdoor activities in New Hampshire. A 161-mile (259-km) stretch of the Appalachian Trail goes through the state.

A hiker pauses to take in the view on top of Mt. Webster in New Hampshire's White Mountain National Forest.

There are many other opportunities to enjoy New Hampshire's wonderful outdoors. Summer activities include camping, canoeing, climbing, biking, boating, hiking, horseback riding, kayaking, and sailing. There are popular swimming beaches along the Atlantic Coast.

Hunting and fishing are state traditions. White-tailed deer are commonly hunted in the state's forests.

New Hampshire is famous for its great skiing and snowboarding areas. Other winter activities include dog sledding, tubing, snowshoeing, ice climbing, ice fishing, and ice skating. There are about 7,000 miles (11,265 km) of snowmobile trails in the state.

A snowboarder goes airborne at the Loon Mountain ski resort's terrain park in Lincoln, New Hampshire.

Entertainment

New Hampshire has a long tradition of fairs and festivals. The Keene Pumpkin Festival

The Keene Pumpkin Festival is held every October.

is known for its lighted jack-o'-lanterns. More than 25,000 pumpkins have filled the town in years past.

The New Hampshire Highland Games are held at Loon Mountain. The festival celebrates Scottish culture. It includes bagpipes and drums, dances, plus heavy athletics and sheepdog competitions.

New Hampshire has many theater companies, orchestras, galleries, and art museums. They include Dartmouth College's Hood Museum of Art and the University of New Hampshire's Museum of Art. There are also many fine historic museums and sites.

Canobie Lake Park is an amusement park near Salem, New Hampshire. It has about 85 rides.

There are several auto-racing tracks in the state. The largest is the New Hampshire Motor Speedway, which hosts NASCAR races.

The NASCAR Sprint Cup Series Sylvania 300 was held at the New Hampshire Motor Speedway in Loudon, New Hampshire.

Timeline

1000 BC—Native Americans create villages and plant crops in the area that will become New Hampshire.

1629—John Mason receives the area between the Merrimack and Piscataqua Rivers and names it New Hampshire.

1741—Benning Wentworth is appointed governor.

1769—Dartmouth College is founded in Hanover, New Hampshire.

1774—American colonists successfully raid Fort William and Mary.

1776—New Hampshire becomes the first state to declare itself independent of Great Britain.

1788—New Hampshire becomes the 9th state.

1808—Concord becomes the state's capital.

1853—New Hampshire native Franklin Pierce becomes U.S. president.

1861-1865—The Civil War. New Hampshire stays in the Union.

1952—New Hampshire establishes the first-in-the-nation presidential primary.

√**2003**—The Old Man of the Mountain, a granite "face" on Cannon Mountain and famous New Hampshire symbol, falls.

Glossary

Civil War—The war fought between America's Northern and Southern states from 1861-1865. The Southern states were for slavery. They wanted to start their own country. Northern states fought against slavery and a division of the country.

Colony—A colony is the establishment of a settlement in a new location. It is often ruled by another country.

Glacier—Huge sheets of ice that grow and shrink when the climate changes. They shape the land beneath them. Long ago, glaciers once covered New Hampshire.

Heavy Athletics—A series of Scottish games that require a great deal of strength. They include the caber (tree trunk) toss and hammer throw.

Industrial Revolution—A period of time starting in the late 1700s when machines began taking over many types of work that before had been done by hand.

Lewis and Clark—Meriwether Lewis and William Clark explored the West from 1804-1806.

Militia—Citizens who help the regular army. They are usually called for service during a military emergency.

NASA (National Aeronautics and Space Administration)—A U.S. government agency started in 1958. NASA's goals include space exploration, as well as increasing people's understanding of Earth, our solar system, and the universe.

New England—An area in the northeast United States, consisting of the states of Maine, Vermont, New Hampshire, Massachusetts, Rhode Island, and Connecticut.

Primary—An election of people called delegates, who choose a political candidate for office.

Privateer—A privately owned and operated warship, which has a government license to attack and capture enemy vessels. The government acts as a partner in the business, receiving a percentage of the profits.

Index